The Art of Basketball War

ANCIENT WISDOM
FOR THE MODERN COACH

MOON TZU

outskirts press

The Art of Basketball War
Ancient Wisdom for the Modern Coach
All Rights Reserved.
Copyright © 2017 Moon Tzu
v2.0

Sun Tzu THE ART OF WAR quotes courtesy of
http://www.artofwarquotes.com/
http://www.goodreads.com/work/quotes/3200649-s-nzi-b-ngf
http://www.military-quotes.com/Sun-Tzu.htm

Outskirts Press, Inc.
http://www.outskirtspress.com

ISBN: 978-1-4787-8184-4

Outskirts Press and the "OP" logo are trademarks belonging to Outskirts Press, Inc.

PRINTED IN THE UNITED STATES OF AMERICA

CONTENTS

INTRODUCTION

The ART OF WAR by Sun Tzu written well over two thousand years ago by a mysterious Chinese warrior-philosopher, is still perhaps the most widely read and influential book of military and business strategy in the world. The book examines strategic principles of conflict on all levels – physical, psychological, emotional and organizational. The wisdom found in this ancient manual can be directly applied to coaching the game of basketball which at its core is nothing more than a battlefield skirmish.

Because basketball is merely a game, there are no life-and-death issues; but if viewed as a beautiful chess match using human pieces, the application of ancient Chinese military strategies will enhance the chances of victory and awaken the impulse to become a more effective leader. The overriding theme of this book is to introduce the parallels between ancient leadership principles and modern coaching philosophy. The following is a quote from a third century Chinese military strategist and devotee of Sun Tzu:

> **The Tao of military operations lies in harmonizing people. When people are in harmony, they will fight naturally, without being exhorted to do so. If the officers and soldiers are suspicious of each other, warriors will not enlist; if loyal advice is not heard, small minds will talk and criticize in secret. When**

hypocrisy sprouts, even if you have the wisdom of ancient warrior kings you could not defeat a peasant, let alone a crowd of them.' Zhuge Liang

The structure of the original text is divided into 13 chapters, each addressing an aspect of organization or battle strategy. This book reflects the same divisions. Each of the thirteen chapters is designed to be intensely practical. The humble observations spring from the battle scars of over a thousand official varsity frays and from the friendly consultation with gray-haired generals who spent their lifetimes leading young men into basketball battle.

 # FLOOR GENERAL

Phog Allen: (career: 1912 - 1956)

Forest Clare Allen, nicknamed Phog because of his fog-horn voice, entered the University of Kansas in 1904, where he lettered three years in basketball under the tutelage of basketball inventor James Naismith. He was instrumental in basketball becoming accepted as an official sport in the Olympics. He coached college basketball for 50 seasons, and compiled a 746–264 record, retiring with the all-time record for most coaching wins in college basketball history at the time. During his tenure at Kansas, Allen coached Dutch Lonborg, Adolph Rupp, Ralph Miller and Dean Smith, all future Hall of Fame coaches. The home basketball arena at the University of Kansas was named in his honor when it opened in 1955. A banner that hangs in the rafters of Allen Fieldhouse reads: "Pay heed all who enter, beware of the Phog."

Regard your soldiers as your children, and they will follow you into the deepest valleys. Look on them as your own beloved sons, and they will stand by you even unto death!

■ *Sun Tzu*

1. CREATING A WARRIOR CULTURE

Four criteria are vital when choosing your soldiers:

1. Competitiveness
2. Coachablity
3. Teachablilty
4. Talent

Having a **competitive** temperament is imperative to athletic success. To be unafraid of failure, to crave the challenge, to relish the struggle, to bask in accomplishment however fleeting and to never be complacent in one's skill development are qualities of character. After a hard loss the leader prefers tears to indifference. After a great victory, a leader prefers unanimous celebration. Thus is the way of the competitor.

A warrior must be **coachable**. He or she must be receptive to instruction and must embrace the expectations and goals set by leadership. Resistance to instruction results in tension, disharmony and dissension in both small and large ways. Sometimes outside voices invade the ears of young warriors. The athlete must suppress the tug of individuality for the greater welfare of the whole.

Every level of sport has increasing degrees of sophistication. The warrior/athlete who is both competitive and coachable must also be **teachable**. If the athlete cannot grasp nor execute important skills or strategies, he or she will impede paths to victory. More importantly, in the words of the great Chinese philosopher Kung Fu Tzu (Confucius) "It is impossible for a person to begin to learn what he thinks he already knows."

The swift, the strong, the agile, the skilled, the **talented** ultimately are predictors of victory. Do not neglect to envision the potential of the unfinished athlete. Always consider the grade in school as well as the team's depth at any given position.

Test of fire: It is prudent to have more than one tryout session in different parts of the year. Upon rare occasion, a candidate who was overlooked can improve significantly through physical growth and skill work, and may prove their mettle during a later "test of fire." Tryouts should be both physically and mentally demanding in order to reveal both the toughness and hunger of all candidates and returning players. In addition, the grueling days of tryouts/practices become a badge of honor, set a competitive tone for the season, and accelerate the process of conditioning for opening night.

Cutting players: Young candidates willingly make themselves vulnerable. If a hopeful was truly on the borderline, be sure to acknowledge his or her effort in some form of face-to-face or written communication. In some cases a coach should request a rec. or church league schedule in order to see the player perform in a different competitive environment.

Tepid soldiers: Be wary of the tepid soldier. The strong general understands the principle of "addition by subtraction." If a returning player is wavering in his desire to be part of the squad, it is prudent for the general to move on with minimal concern once honest communication has ended. A campaign is best executed with soldiers who share a deep and common commitment. Cool water refreshes; warm water is spit out.

The warrior mentality: The effective general must be perceived by his troops as blindly committed to victory. He or she must plunge fearlessly into the abyss for it is the leader who sets the tone for the entire program. What is your team identity? How is your team regarded by your enemies? What would be the first words on the opponent's scouting report to describe your troops - tenacious, relentless, intelligent, disciplined, stingy, hard-nosed, patient? - or chaotic, sloppy, predictable, careless, selfish, inconsistent, soft?

Honestly answer these questions about your squad – "Who are we? What do we stand for?" Create a culture of accountability. Create a culture where the older players model and teach the younger ones. Insist on loud and constant verbal encouragement from teammates. Create a culture that minimizes "game slippage" by demanding that every practice drill be performed at game speed.

US	NOT US
Loose ball diving	Ref blaming
Charge taking	Finger pointing
Verbals screaming	Trash talking
Offensive board crashing	Stat padding
Box out holding	Cheap shot taking
Free throw making	Jersey popping
Teammate encouraging	Laurel resting

Locker room: A squad's locker room should be a sanctuary. Ninety percent of team socialization takes place there. Make sure it reflects your program's pride. Demand that it be respected. Create a winner's ambiance through quotes, posters, articles, banners, trophies, wall art, glory blocks (totems of great wins).

Staying relevant: The game is always progressing. Younger generals are reshaping, retooling, advancing, inventing, implementing better technology and consulting newer resources. Like the oak, the veteran leader must stand firm in enforcing core values, but like the supple pine in tempestuous gales must bend to prevent uprooting. The wise leader stays current, stays open, stays pliable, stays in touch with youthful trends or he will eventually fade to irrelevance.

Having favorites: The effective leader does not play favorites, but it is impossible not to have favorites. Below are ten ways a player becomes a coach's favorite:

1. Arrives early. Stays late.

2. Generates energy and enthusiasm in practice.

3. Pays attention in the huddle. Listens with his/her eyes.

4. Cheers for his/her teammates when not in the game.

5. Is polite to those who can be of no use to him/her.

6. Does the dirty jobs of winning – defense, charges, sprinting back on defense.

7. Never makes an excuse – accepts corrections with eye contact and a nod.

8. Isn't a clown or jerk in the locker room.

9. Isn't a distraction in the class room. Teachers make it a point to initiate compliments about the player's behavior and performance.

10. Hits the winning shot against your biggest rival!

FLOOR GENERAL

Clair Bee: (career: 1925-1954)

Known as the "Innovator" for creating the 1-3-1 zone defense, advocating for the 3-second rule, and helping the NBA develop the 24-second shot clock, Clair Bee led **Long Island University** to two undefeated seasons and two National Invitational Tournament titles in 1939 and 1941 when the NCAA was still in its infancy. He was also a prolific writer, penning more than 20 + juvenile sports fiction books in the "Chip Hilton" series, which is considered one of the most influential sports fiction series ever written.

When the common soldiers are too strong and their officers too weak, the result is INSUBORDINATION. When the officers are too strong and the common soldiers too weak, the result is COLLAPSE. When the higher officers are angry and insubordinate, and on meeting the enemy give battle on their own account from a feeling of resentment, before the commander-in-chief can tell whether or not he is in a position to fight, the result is RUIN.

■ *Sun Tzu*

2. MILITARY ORGANIZATION

Do not give orders that can be understood. Give orders that cannot be misunderstood! (General Douglas MacArthur)

The effective general excels in clear communication. Clarity of commands benefit the entire organization. A basketball regiment includes not only the coaching staff and players, but an array of ancillary participants – managers, statisticians, videographers, scorekeepers, cheerleaders, bus drivers, administrators, concessionaires, boosters and parents.

All generals value loyal officers. The worth of a talented assistant is incalculable. When trust is confirmed, the time comes to delegate crucial areas of command. Groom your assistants to be capable of assuming full command in your absence. Employ former players. They have a profound understanding of your system and a deep personal investment in the program; however, there are also countless benefits to including coaches from other programs. Fresh drills, fresh questions, fresh insight can strengthen areas of weakness. The enlightened general seeks advice then weighs the advantages or disadvantages of the suggestions. Once the decision is rendered the officers must embrace its implementation and resist any desire for public credit. More importantly if the strategy is unsuccessful, the staff should embark on a healthy analysis. Any **public** second- guessing by a subordinate is tantamount to treason.

Officers are a natural conduit for unhappy players, parents and fans. The trusted assistant must filter what is important before bringing the matter to the general. Assistants must be aware that sympathetic ears are as water sprinkled on weeds.

Also, players are prone to reveal events from their private lives more freely to younger officers. The general should be informed of any situations that may imperil the well-being of the player or the welfare of the team.

Basic division of duties:

Head coach:

1. Coach the coaches
2. Sync personal philosophies with athletic director, administrators and school mission statements.
3. Be attentive to feeder programs, but do not micro-manage.
4. Build healthy public relations – written media, radio, TV, fans, faculty, parents.
5. Be responsible for general team discipline and conduct.
6. Monitor academic progress of all players.
7. Develop daily practice plans
8. Devise detailed game plans
9. Counsel
10. Ensure that coach-player relationships extend post-grad.

Assistant coaches:

1. Become the consummate expert for teaching the fundamentals of your assigned areas: post players, point guards, shooting drills, out of bounds plays, scout team, zones, presses.
2. Coordinate video scouting - communicate exchanges, update email distribution and passwords, try to identify what is not obvious.
3. Supervise the managers, statisticians, video crew.
4. Assist in strength and conditioning.
5. Analyze statistics at half time, post-game, post season.

6. Participate in practice planning.

7. Participate in game planning.

8. Provide effective bulletin board material.

9. Help to create off-season individual player development programs.

10. Coach the team's pre-game warm-ups to ensure complete focus.

FLOOR GENERAL

Hank Iba: (career: 1929-1970)

Known as "the Iron Duke of Defense," he was a strict discipli-
narian and regarded as a coaching martinet. Iba's **Oklahoma
State** teams won two national championships. His teams were
methodical, ball-control units that featured weaving patterns
and low scoring games. The first thing Iba would do each season would be to tell his players, "We're not going to play
them; they're going to play us." Iba's "swinging gate" defense
was the prototype for future *pack-line* man-to-man principles.
Iba coached the USA Olympic basketball team in 1964, 1968
and 1972. He is the first coach in USA Olympic basketball
history to coach two gold medal winning teams - 1964 in
Tokyo and 1968 in Mexico City. In 1987, OSU's home arena,
Gallagher Hall, was renamed Gallagher-Iba Arena in Iba's
honor. A seat in the southeast concourse level of the arena
is known as "Mr. Iba's Seat," which remains empty during
games.

Maneuvering with an army is advantageous; with an undisciplined multitude, most dangerous.

■ *Sun Tzu*

3. DISCIPLINE IN DRILL AND PRACTICE

Battles are won in practice. The tone, the pace, the sequencing of drills and the selection of emphasis ultimately determine the consistency of excellence throughout the season. There will always be battles throughout the season that generate inspired combat with little or no coaching input. Rivalry games and grudge matches take care of themselves. It is those mid-week, poorly attended skirmishes that can often be stolen by the squadron whose practice habits involve a systematic insistence on perfect fundamentals and game-speed effort.

Prescribe a pre-practice ritual that players must perform when they step on the practice floor – it should involve elements to warm the muscles (jogging, pivoting, ball-slapping, jump stopping), stretching, ball handling, dribbling, form shooting, live ball moves. Aimless, lazy shooting and pointless fraternizing must be discouraged. Coaches should be on the floor supervising, inspecting and participating in player development.

Encourage the discipline of *2 speeds* - Players must run/jog everywhere or if they are absolutely too tired to run/jog, they must stand still. In other words discourage all "walking." This habit transfers to an over-all perception of purposeful movement on game nights. The team that hustles to the bench when a time-out is called will maximize instruction time.

Encourage the discipline of **+ 1**. When a player is asked to perform a corrective discipline (push-up, air toe- touch) he/she will always do one more than required.

When a drill instructor blows his/her whistle, all shooting must immediately stop. No errant balls should hit the floor.

These small disciplines, if rigorously enforced, help to create a unified mindset. Eventually, the players themselves will police these expectations.

Sequence of drills: Incorporate continuity offenses, sets, and delay games as part of the troop's warm-up regimen. All players are moving briskly, and reinforcing the timing of the offenses.

The least favorite part of the game for most players is defense. The prudent staff will include a gradation of defensive drills early in each practice. The message becomes embedded that defense is priority Number One. Begin with footwork fundamentals then eventually build to 5 on 5 full court scrimmage.

When doing half-court work, frequently change ends of the court for freshness and variety.

Incorporate numerous high-rep shooting drills in every practice. Shooting is absolutely the MOST IMPORTANT skill for every fighting unit, yet it is often under-emphasized in practice planning.

Foul shooting pressure can never be perfectly simulated, but the clever drill sergeant always creates some form of stakes in every foul shooting drill. The rebounders should always make the return pass to the shooter with their weak hand (the savvy young cadet will build a few 'weak hand' dribbles into his foul shot routine. He/she will get thousands of more reps that way).

FLOOR GENERAL

John Mclendon: (career: 1936-1970)

Considered the father of modern basketball, Coach McClendon was a basketball and civil rights pioneer. A supreme innovator, teacher and consummate gentleman Coach McLendon was the first African-American coach to be inducted into the Naismith Memorial Hall of Fame. He captured three consecutive NAIA national championships at **Tennessee A&I**. His commitment to speeding up the pace of basketball by employing fast break and pressure defense techniques helped to usher in an exciting style of play that radically departed from the slow, deliberate pace of the game. Coach McClendon once described the role of the coach as "the syrup in a bottle of coca-cola. The drink is 98% fizzle water and only 2% syrup, but without the syrup you don't have a coke."

If you know the enemy and know yourself, you need not fear the result of a hundred battles . . . unless you know the mountains and forests, the defiles and impasses, and the lay of the marshes and swamps, you cannot maneuver with an armed force.

■ *Sun Tzu*

4. RECONNAISSANCE OF THE ENEMY

The most important factor in battlefield preparation is to eliminate the element of surprise. The prudent general uses every resource available to amass information regarding the enemy's strengths, weaknesses, tendencies, state of preparedness, health, history and recent strategies. Obtain statistics from at least three of the opponents' most recent games to track the current rotation and leading scorers. Obtain video through on-line services to gauge size and speed, assess tempo, determine defensive schemes, detect favorite go-to sets, and end-of-quarter strategies. Pay particular attention to backdoor cues, under the basket out-of-bounds plays, switching tendencies, as well as when and where the opponent may employ traps or presses. Take notice of which players are one handed dribblers and prone to turnover pressure, which players are effective penetrators, and which shoulder a big man favors. Never be unaware of a proficient outside shooter who comes off an opponent's bench. Determine how to disrupt any delay game offense. Pay attention to an opponent's alignment for entering the ball from the sideline. You may be able to create a critical turnover by switching or jumping a pass.

Speak directly to coaches who have already gone to war with your upcoming opponent. Ask them to send their scouting report if they are willing to share it. Many in the coaching fraternity will oblige if you reciprocate. Special insights can be gleaned by reading another army's evaluation of the threat.

Commit your scouting observations to written form for distribution to your troops. Make sure to include what each opposing player can do to thwart your team's goals. Predict how they will attack and defend your team.

Film work is critical to familiarizing your team with the opponent, however, do it through clips. Do not spend endless time in the film room with your team. They learn best by the physical movement on the court.

Your scout team should work on only a few of the most unfamiliar and dangerous hits or sets. This ensures that they are simulated with some degree of precision. Preparing for too many eventualities dilutes the process. If your defensive philosophy is built on sound principles of communication, help, and anticipation; you can be confident they will handle just about any situation that arises.

Still, the most reliable scouting reconnaissance strategy is personal eyewitness. If at all possible the commanding general should observe opponent clashes first hand. Innumerable revelations result from observing huddles, overhearing the names of set plays being called, observing hand signals, noticing substitution patterns, interpreting body language and speaking with the occasional loose-lipped fan who might divulge a detail of interest.

Finally, in high school contests most JV games are played prior to the varsity game. In 98% of all programs, the sets and calls are exactly the same as the varsity. JV players are a great source of scouting material and should have their antennas up to capture and confirm enemy secrets.

FLOOR GENERAL

Tex Winter: (career: 1940-2008)

Considered the premier authority on the Triangle Offense, Tex Winter trained as a fighter pilot during World War II. Winter returned to college after the war enrolling at the University of Southern California, where he learned the Triangle Offense from his coach Sam Barry. Winter was named UPI National Coach of the Year in 1958 after he led **Kansas State** to the Final Four by knocking off Oscar Robertson and second-ranked Cincinnati in an 83-80 double-overtime thriller. In 1985, Winter started his tenure as an assistant coach with the **Chicago Bulls** under Phil Jackson implementing the triangle offense which helped to produce six NBA championships. He added three more rings as an assistant to Jackson with the **Los Angeles Lakers**.

All warfare is based on deception. Hence, when able to attack, we must seem unable; when using our forces, we must seem inactive; when we are near, we must make the enemy believe we are far away; when far away, we must make him believe we are near. Hold out baits to entice the enemy. Feign disorder, and crush him.

■ *Sun Tzu*

5. BATTLE STRATEGIES

Every head fake, jab step, v-cut, back door, pass fake, crossover, change of pace, slipped screen and charge involves deception. Whether an army chooses to press and trap, or sag and switch, the object is to lure the opponent into mistakes and frustration. The audacious general takes advantage of misdirection and subterfuge to gain an advantage.

Changing defenses for at least one possession coming out of a time-out called by the opponent can interrupt flow, create some chaos and disrupt an opponent's comfort level. Stay in the new defense at least until one basket is scored against it.

Simply by changing a zone from a 2-front to a 1-front can present some problems for the attack strategy of an opponent. In some cases it can patch some leaks in your own fortress.

Foul counts- The seasoned leader will gamble on the odds of a player fouling out. A player's presence on the floor contributes more significantly to the victory than saving him from the unlikely event of disqualification. Remove a player after he/she commits two fouls in the 1st quarter or gets his third in the 2nd quarter. If he/she gets a fourth foul in the 3rd quarter keep them on the bench until the five-minute mark of the 4th. On very rare occasions this strategy can backfire, but veterans of pitched battles agree on this philosophy.

Script the first three offensive plays of a game. It takes pressure off the point guard.

It is ideal that in the first possession of a game all players touch the ball in a continuity flow in order to get oriented to the spotlight and stimulate the tactile nerve endings.

Half time is for hydration, evaluation and anticipation. Always prepare them for the unexpected. Mention possible surprise strategies they may confront (presses, gimmicks, handoff traps).

Sometimes commanders miss some details from their bench vantage points. Ask the players what they are noticing out there on the floor. There may be some breakdowns in communication that need remedied.

It is well-known that the first three minutes of the second half can determine the battle's outcome. Be disciplined in returning your team to the floor after half-time. Make sure they have a productive re-warmup period.

Upon occasion a general should take a non-traditional approach to half-time adjustments and corrections. Keep the players on the floor to run offenses (especially if injury, foul trouble or sickness has forced players to play unfamiliar positions), out-of-bounds plays, shooting drills, ball-handling drills or team defensive adjustments. This 15 minute mini-practice might fine-tune some offensive or defensive timing as well as jolt the team into deeper focus.

On the initial possession of the second half, choose a 'go-to' play that pounds the ball inside resulting in a basket or a foul. This can often set the tone and re-ignite the effort level.

Always call two plays coming out of a timeout – 1 man, 1 zone.

With six seconds or less, the prudent general will instruct his team to foul if they are up by 3 points. There are overwhelming statistics to support this. The number of games that have been lost because a three-pointer sent the game into overtime vs. the number of games that have been lost by the improbable combination of freak bounces during free throws is staggering.

When an opponent scores the go-ahead basket with 5 seconds or more, combatants should not call time out. Enter the ball immediately and push the ball up court to take advantage of the opponent's celebratory chaos.

Always practice end-of-game situations with a variety of line-ups. Your long-pass in-bounder should have a dependable understudy as well.

If your long-pass in-bounder is injured and unable to compete, but can still execute that one skill, put him/her in uniform just in case that critical situation arises.

Make sure you have a half-court trapping defense to prevent another team from holding the ball at the end of a game.

If your tallest players can make 3-pointers, design opportunities for them. The value of 3-point baskets far outweighs the occasional offensive rebound that they get planted in the paint.

Play your best five basketball players together regardless of size. Do not be afraid to go small.

 **FLOOR GENERAL**

Pete Newell: (career: 1946-1960)

Considered "America's Basketball Guru," Pete Newell was one of the most influential coaches in the history of basketball. He is one of only three coaches to win the "Triple Crown" of NIT, NCAA and Olympic championships. He won the NIT in 1949 at **San Francisco University**, an NCAA championship at the **University of California** in 1959 and an Olympic championship in 1960. His *Big-Man* camp became a required seminar in low-post play for hundreds of professional players. Other contributions to the game include his "Reverse Action Offense," a continuity flow that attacks from both sides of the court, and his stall strategy, called "Three Out, Two In," designed to protect a lead. This predated the similar "four corners" technique popularized by Dean Smith at North Carolina.

Even if opponents are numerous they can be made not to fight... All we need to do is throw something odd and unaccountable in their way.

■ *Sun Tzu*

6. DEFEATING SUPERIOR FORCES

The psychology of the upset revolves around two factors:

1. Fear must be replaced by a vision of great opportunity. The enlightened general will frame the battle as an opportunity for glory, an opportunity to reveal extraordinary traits of character.
2. A game plan should be prepared with meticulous detail and presented to the troops with complete conviction.

Commitment to the following are imperative in any great victory:

1. Limiting the opponent to one shot, box-out fanaticism and gang rebounding.

2. Sprinting back in defensive transition. Never allowing an imbalance in offensive numbers.

3. Giving early help on all penetration.

4. Minimizing turnovers.

5. Being fearless in taking charges.

The game MUST be shortened. A team with truly superior weapons must be held to fewer offensive possessions. This allows the underdog to stay within striking distance in the critical minutes when a momentum shift can turn the tide to victory.

The shrewd general can dictate tempo both defensively and offensively. Offensive patience can frustrate superior teams who are used to high volume scoring with minimal time on defense. Make a high scoring team play long stretches of defense, and they become careless and mistake prone. Furthermore, the opponent tends to rush their offense when they do gain possession of the ball.

Running a continuity offense a few times before attacking creates a diversion (faux offense). Spreading the floor in 4-corners creates consternation. Blend the two strategies to shake the confidence of enemy officers who've grown complacent in their arrogance.

When a shot clock is involved, concentrate on making the point guard work extra hard to get the ball inbounds. After a score, immediately find and face guard. Force him up the sideline to be met by a second defender (the man guarding the in-bounder who hovers a little deeper near the foul line).

This often forces a pass back to the in-bounder who is generally not comfortable with the ball and will expend several more seconds trying to get it back to the point guard.

Employ a floating ¾ court press to slow the ball's advancement by requiring ball reversals which helps to push the opponent deeper into the shot clock each time down.

Never be afraid to use a gimmick defense. A 'box and one' (1-3 chaser) or a 'triangle and two' can be tremendous equalizers vs. superior forces. Forcing responsibilities on weaker warriors can bring great benefits. Opponent forces must figure out new attack points in real time. Few units will have effectively prepared for this tactic. Their shots will come from uncomfortable spots, penetrators will get bottled up, and predictable scorers will get neutralized.

If a key opponent gets in foul trouble, call plays that subject him/her to a charge call – hand-off into a high pick, blind back-screen, post criss-cross. Flop like fish until the rule gets enforced.

Shot selection: No shot should be squandered. Shots should be taken in rhythm with a reasonable chance of being rebounded or recovered. Of course, the time on the clock and the score of the game dictate the merit of any shot.

Handling pressure: Invariably, a proud enemy with a history of victory will become desperate when sensing defeat. Be sure to prepare and instill confidence in all press-breaking and trap breaking strategies. For like the wild boar cornered by dogs, an opponent will attack with a sense of urgent self-preservation.

 **FLOOR GENERAL**

Ed McCluskey: (career: 1948 – 1976)

Coach Ed McCluskey is a Pennsylvania high school coaching legend. He began coaching at Farrell High School in 1948 winning 590 games in 29 seasons while losing only 153, a winning percentage of more than 80. His seven Pennsylvania state 'Big School' crowns are still the standard in state basketball history. His teams gained a reputation for playing tenacious man-to-man defense coupled with a highly disciplined "open post motion offense." Considered one of the great basketball minds of the 20th century, legions of young coaches borrowed his drills, studied his practice organization and adopted a similar coaching philosophy. One of Farrell's most celebrated wins was a 1954 victory over Philadelphia Overbrook High School led by their seven foot senior phenom Wilt Chamberlain. Farrell handed Overbrook its only loss of the season.

Rapidity is the essence of war: take advantage of the enemy's unreadiness, make your way by unexpected routes, and attack unguarded spots.

■ *Sun Tzu*

7. AVOIDING AMBUSH BY INFERIOR ARMIES

The experienced general accepts full responsibility for his troop's physical and mental preparation for combat. When confronted with a dangerous "trap game" or encountering an army that was previously routed by your forces, the psychological edge can be dulled. No fighting force can muster and sustain optimal performance in every single fray throughout a campaign; however, the army that consistently approaches the highest standard of competitiveness night in and night out will avoid embarrassing defeats at untimely points in the fighting season. The ancient adage "you play like you practice" is a sagacious observation. A squad's game-effort should be governed by habit not emotion.

Plant seeds: When an underestimated enemy appears on the horizon, the wise leader will embed small warnings and reminders of the peril that looms even when preparing for another opponent. Direct references to a style of play, a key player, a recent conquest, or league standings help to lodge an awareness of the upset potential of an impending opponent.

Introduce something new: The crafty general can awaken new enthusiasm in battle preparation by adding a new play to the repertoire. Provide a quick hitter, a back door play, a new wrinkle in an offensive set to heighten focus and stimulate anticipation.

Full court press: Trap games are a good time to "come out swinging" by starting in a full court press. Your soldiers are jolted into hustle-mode early when they have fresh legs. The ambush can be successful if the defenders will clamp all traps with quickness and commitment.

Substitution patterns: Sometimes tinkering with substitution patterns and player combinations injects some freshness to the battle's flow. The astute general may also discover some revealing insights into younger cadets who may be ready for promotion.

Indirect verbal motivation: When a fighting unit seems un-ready for combat before a skirmish with an inferior opponent, the commander should manufacture something that upsets him that may be seemingly unrelated to the contest at hand (classroom behavior, academic effort, punctuality, inappro-priate on-line media activity etc). A well-timed, high decibel lashing right before a contest can upon occasion jump-start the focus that is lacking.

If a squad's effort and execution were uninspired, the general must at least privately assume his/her share of the blame; however, in the binary reality of sports, there are only two possible outcomes so a "bad win" cannot exist. Thus is the wisdom of the ancient masters.

FLOOR GENERAL

Pat Head Summitt (career: 1974-2012)

Pat Head Summit is the only person in America to have two Division I basketball courts named in her honor – **The University of Tennessee-Martin** where she played, and **The University of Tennesee-Knoxville** where she coached. In 1974, Trish (Patricia) Head was hired as the head coach of the University of Tennessee at the age of 22. Two years later she represented the United States as a member of the 1976 Olympic basketball team. No one has been more instrumental in popularizing and legitimizing women's college basketball than Coach Summitt. To her peers, she was a respected, ethical, competitive winner whose teams set a standard of excellence both on the floor and in the classroom. To the public she was an intense, demanding and focused leader who served as the sport's greatest ambassador. Her junior high school coach and phys. ed instructor Joe Daves recalled having to administer corporal punishment to a young Trish Head for using a mini-trampoline in an attempt to dunk the ball after a gym class. This behavior was strictly forbidden by class rules. He quipped years later that he was the only coach in America who ever truly "whupped" Coach Summitt's butt on a basketball floor.

Do not be afraid to send your troops into a positon from which there is no retreat . . . The momentum of skilled warriors is like a round boulder tumbling down a thousand-foot mountain.

■ *Sun Tzu*

8. THE ART OF THE COMEBACK

All seasoned generals have experienced battles in which heavy losses seem to doom the outcome early on. When an opponent seizes the upper-hand and seems destined for victory, the tide of battle can be reversed through the sheer force of will of the combatants who must maintain an unquestioning belief in the decisions of their general.

Shifting momentum plays a part in nearly every confrontation, and the savvy general senses how to seize and extend it for the benefit of his troops. Great and glorious come-backs will often enter the folklore of a community's oral and written tradition.

Half-time deficit: If an army finds themselves down by staggering numbers at half-time, a general should address three key points:

1. It took a long time for the deficit to be created. It will take a long time for it to be erased. Just keep chipping away.

2. Wipe away the score. It's now zero to zero. Demand that they win the second half (or else).

3. When the deficit reaches 10 or less, there will be psychological magic.

Tempo: When behind by significant numbers, increase the tempo on both ends of the floor. Create possessions by causing turnovers and forcing quicker shots. Attack with full and half court pressure, scrambling jump and runs, or initial-pass double teams with rotation. Close traps, tip passes, back tap dribblers, take gambles on the back of presses. Get the ball out of the hands of the opponent's best playmaker and don't let him get it back. Institute a no-layup rule when on defense. This would apply to defenders who are not in foul trouble, or who can afford to be. Make the opponent earn his points from the foul line. It stops the clock.

Push the ball up quickly when the opponent scores. Make the inbound pass further down the court instead of near the baseline. This may save several valuable seconds in the long run.

On offense emphasize aggressive penetration to draw fouls which stops the clock. It also forces defenders to sink off your 3-point marksmen.

Even though the 3-point shot is a beautiful weapon to close the scoring gap, too many squads <u>exclusively</u> shoot the three way too early in a comeback and will often rush long, contested shots.

Strategic timeouts: Sometimes, even in the middle of a spirited momentum change a wise general will sense the energy drain and call a time out just to rest his warriors so that the effort can be sustained. Make it a habit to save timeouts for late game clock stoppage after a score to make defensive substitutions and set up the press.

Most teams start to intentionally foul too late. Do not wait until intentional fouls simply pad the opponent's lead. Make sure there is a clear hand signal or verbal command that triggers the intentional foul strategy. Practice this skill to avoid penalty.

There are three desperate strategies to consider during the final seconds of a comeback when the team is out of timeouts.

1. As the ball enters the net, a player can swat the ball out of bounds away from the opponent's in-bounder. The referee will blow his whistle to issue a warning which stops the clock. It will not restart until the ball is entered by the opponent. This ploy can preserve precious seconds.
2. With 5 seconds or less and down 1-3 points, the opponent does not have to enter the ball after a score. Have a defender intentionally step across the end-line and strip the ball from the in-bounder's hands. This will result in a technical foul and give your team at least one more chance to get a 5-second count or steal in the half court.

3. When an opponent is shooting a critical last minute foul shot, instruct the two nearest players to step into the lane directly in front of the shooter in order to obstruct the shot. In the confusion, the foul shooter may pass the ball to the nearest referee. This now constitutes a double violation and the possession is then determined by the arrow.

FLOOR GENERAL

Pete Carril: (career: 1954-2011)

"The strong take from the weak, but the smart take from the strong." This wisdom was imparted to Coach Carril by his immigrant father who worked in a Bethlehem, PA steel mill for thirty-nine years. Pete Carril saw the future of basketball. Inventor of the Princeton Offense, this legendary coach pushed his teams to space the court, pass the ball and shoot 3-pointers. According to Coach Carril, "nothing creates more problems for the defense than movement." The Princeton Offense relies on constant motion and specific counters based on defensive reads. The classic back door cut for an easy basket is its signature option. Pete Carril's coaching journey included positions as a JV high school coach for four years, a head high school coach for eight years, a head college coach for thirty years, and various stints as an NBA assistant.

It is lucky when the rulers nourish the ruled (the I-Ching) . . . Assess the advantages of advice then structure your forces accordingly.

■ *Sun Tzu*

9. EVALUATION AND IMPROVEMENT

Both commanders and warriors must constantly strive to become more proficient and knowledgeable in their crafts. It is incumbent on those who command to become mentors, to model and to 'show the way.' It is incumbent on those who are ruled to be open as a vessel to be filled. Each skirmish, each foray, each battle hides secrets for future conquests. The prudent general reflects and corrects. The honorable warrior increases his strength and prowess through dedicated repetition.

Always **inspect** what you **expect.** This ancient wisdom describes perhaps the most important leadership ethic of all. Leaders do not blame, project or rationalize. They anticipate and prepare their troops for all combat conditions. If a breakdown in execution occurs, there was a breakdown in preparation and communication.

Notebooks: Learning is enhanced and ingrained when information is written down. Knowledge that travels down the arm onto paper deepens more indelibly in the folds of memory. Making your troops record post-game observations has significant benefits. A litany of both corrections and praise serves to crystallize the evaluation. Also, by recording important details of the game while the memory is fresh, the fighting force now has an excellent resource to consult for a return engagement. Notebooks can also be used during film sessions and pre-game meetings.

Post-game analysis: Modern analytics are transforming the game and now play a critical role in team and individual assessment. The more a general understands the metrics, the more informed his battlefield preparation will be. The following are a handful of criteria that merit attention:

Possessions per Game - How many times per game does a team get the ball? The more times your team gets the ball, the more points your team has the opportunity to score.

Points per Possession - How many points does a team score per possession? 1's, 2's, 3's, 'And 1's'

Turnover Percentage - What percentage of possessions does a team give the ball away before they create an opportunity to score.

Effective Field Goal Percentage - How many points does a team score per shot taken from the field?

Free Throw Rate - How many opportunities does a team create to score from the free throw line relative to the number of shots it takes from the field?

Offensive Rebounding Percentage - What percentage of offensive rebounds does a team retrieve which then extends the offensive possession?

Regardless of the depth of analytics that inform a staff, the following reveal the simplest assessment of most game outcomes:

1. Effort (subjective grade)
2. Differentiation in offensive rebounds
3. Differentiation in fast break points
4. Differentiation in turnovers
5. Differentiation in free throws attempted and percent made (a simple team goal should be to make more free throws than the opponent attempts – this generally indicates aggressive offense and disciplined defense)
6. Shot chart ratios - What percent of shots were attempted from team hot spots. All teams have different strengths, so this statistic is fluid from year to year. Some teams demand more inside touches, some teams are more three point dangerous.

   (Ignore shooting percentages from the floor if the team's shot selection was acceptable. Like the vagaries of weather sometimes it rains, sometimes there's a blue sky)

Post-season soldier evaluation: After the season, the prudent general should conduct a face to face and/or written evaluation for each returning soldier. Highlight positive attributes of skill and attitude, and provide specific areas of improvement. Consider not only fundamentals, but practice habits, commitment to defense, decision making, strength goals, and overall basketball I.Q.

Officer input: Allow some time to elapse before conducting an evaluation of the year with your full staff. The meeting will then produce a more objective assessment of both the successes and failures of the last campaign. Use this meeting to discuss changes in the schedule, player development, team chemistry and tweaks to offensive and defensive schemes to maximize the blend of up-coming talent.

Let the fields lie fallow: Allow the nutrients to return to the soil. Allow for some distance before re-engagement. Encourage players to hear other voices, to train and explore with different drills, to be part of other teams. The troops will be hungry and eager to re-deploy when the time comes.

FLOOR GENERAL

Dick Bennett (career: 1965-2006)

In 2002, when the Kohl Center was under construction on the University of Wisconsin campus, Coach Dick Bennett requested permission to bury a laminated card in the foundation. The following five words were written on this card: HUMILITY, PASSION, UNITY, SERVANTHOOD, THANKFULNESS. He told his team that these qualities are the foundation of the Wisconsin basketball program and now symbolically they are part of the foundation of this new building. Dick Bennett's most significant contribution to the body of basketball progress is the PACK-LINE DEFENSE. Developed over countless seasons as a high school, NAIA, and NCAA Division I coach, the pack-line in its purest form presents challenges to every man-to-man offense. Designed to negate effective penetration, eliminate low-post scoring through double teams, and provide excellent rebounding position, this defense has been adopted by programs across the country at every level.

He will win whose army is animated by the same spirit throughout all its ranks.

■ *Sun Tzu*

10. MORALE AND MOTIVATION

The genius of any commander is in his talent to motivate his warriors. Natural leaders always have a finger on the pulse of the troop's morale. Great generals have great instincts and cultivate loyalty and the fighting spirit through vision, enthusiasm, consistency and authenticity.

Team bonding: Nothing bonds like shared suffering. Soldiers who have trained together with challenging rigor, who have fought beside each other in frenzied combat, who have wept and rejoiced together, who have defied all odds, who have rung out every bead of sweat – they are grafted together in brotherhood.

Design a demanding strength and conditioning program. Structure early season practices to include drills that exceed game exhaustion. Inspire pride in your program through the collective effort to achieve excellence. *"Those who work the hardest are the last to surrender."* (anonymous). When the work is done, there will always be time for levity that is the glue for lasting relationships.

Team survey: Develop a written survey form to discover if your perceptions of the squadron match theirs. This exercise creates awareness and reinforces shared values of the group.

1. Who should take the last shot in a tight game?
2. Who is the team's best defensive stopper?
3. Who is the most mentally tough on the team?
4. Who is the team's best free throw shooter?
5. Who would win an Ultimate Fighter tournament among the team?
6. Who will lead the team in charges?
7. Who is the best pure shooter?
8. Who works the hardest in practice?
9. Who has the highest basketball I.Q.
10. Who does the team most respect in regard to character?

Travel: Soldiers are forced out of their comfort zones and often develop new and deeper relationships when presented with different travel experiences. Find ways to compete in new and different environments.

Charity work: Do charity work together – adopt-a-highway, homeless shelter, old folk's home, read to pre-schoolers.

Image: Look sharp, play sharp. Dress for success. Allow the troops to make decisions that you don't care about – uniform design, travel gear, practice gear, weekend practice times.

New gear: Surprise the team with a new set of uniforms at mid-year once in a cycle.

Weekly inter-squad fall newsletter: An informal weekly publication counting down the days until the first official practice can build anticipation and help solidify the team culture. Consider including the following:

1. Workout observations.
2. Pick-up game critiques.
3. Football commentary – school, college, pro.
4. League predictions for upcoming basketball season.
5. Rumors of transfers or coaching changes.
6. New wrinkles in offense or defense.
7. Twitter quotes.
8. Inspirational stories.
9. Memories of last season triumphs or nightmares.
10. Players to watch in the league.

Big vivids: When a battle looms that requires a special psychological edge, the superior general should provide a dramatic stimulus to enhance team cohesion.

The internet is rife with inspirational sports videos that tout the virtues of hard work and the resulting defiance of impossible odds.

Invite a speaker of special status to address the troops to provide personal insight.

Rent a local theater for a chartered viewing of a current relatable movie.

Create an anonymous scouting report on your team. Use tepid praise for strengths (both individual and team), and exaggerate exposure of weaknesses. (Some generals use the ruse of placing an opponent's logo at the top and claiming it was found in an opponent's locker room.)

FLOOR GENERAL

Morgan Wooten: (career: 1951-2002)

Universally recognized as the nation's greatest high school basketball coach, Morgan Wooten began his career as a baseball coach at **Saint Joseph's Home for Boys** in Washington, D.C., where he went 0-16; however, in his forty-six years at **DeMatha Catholic** (1956 -2002) his basketball teams amassed 1,274 wins with only 192 defeats. Wooten is credited with many of the innovations now common in competitive basketball. His DeMatha team was one of the first to play powerhouses from other states, to use full-court pressure defenses and to craft defensive techniques that lead to the offensive foul (charge). He emphatically emphasized proper fundamentals and developed drills to perfect live-ball one-on-one moves. In 1965, DeMatha ended the 71-game winning streak of New York City powerhouse Power Memorial, which was led by 7-2 center Lew Alcindor, who later became Kareem Abdul-Jabbar. The game was a sellout at the University of Maryland's Cole Field House.

If, however, you are too soft and do not establish firm leadership, and do not enforce your orders, if you are lax in your organization and cannot keep control – then your troops will be as useless to you as spoilt children.

■ *Sun Tzu*

11. NON - NEGOTIABLES

A military leader will always settle for what he is willing to tolerate; therefore, set high standards in great things and small. Soldiers appreciate and even crave discipline, order and clarity. These virtues contribute most to victory and survival. Without being arbitrary or petty, determine what on-court and off-court behaviors will be enforced with no flexibility. Below are a collection of some standard non-negotiables employed by successful generals.

On-court:

Jogging to huddles at timeouts.

Using the board on all layups.

Jump stops to prevent traveling.

Over-the-head soccer inbound passes (rarely get tipped).

Defensive communication using verbals.

An attentive and engaged bench (5 guys on the floor, but 12 guys in the game).

No vanity displays (Aside from uncommon competitive effort, do nothing additional to bring attention to yourself.)

Helping a teammate up from the floor.

Off-court :

Punctuality for all team events

Clean locker room

Notifying head coach if sick or if an emergency prevents practice attendance.

Inappropriate social media behavior

Inappropriate class room behavior

Team rules: The fewer rules the better. Most negative conduct that requires attention by officers requires a review of circumstances and context; therefore, it is wise to list a gradation of possible consequences i.e. – punishment may include physical punishment, game suspension or dismissal depending on the frequency and degree of the offense.

 **FLOOR GENERAL**

Don Meyer: (career: 1967-2010)

Coach Don Meyer had three inviolable rules for his team, staff, campers and counselors: 1. Everybody takes notes. 2. Everybody says "please and thank you." 3. Everybody picks up trash. Although he coached at three small colleges (Hamline, Lipscomb, Northern State), Coach Meyer is universally acclaimed as one of the game's greatest teachers. Some of basketball's most prominent coaches have paid homage to his knowledge and influence including Bob Knight, Mike Krzyzewski, Pat Summitt and John Wooden. What he loved about coaching was to see improvement in players both on the court and as people. When he wasn't busy winning games, Meyer was producing instructional videotapes, conducting youth and coaching clinics or speaking to business and civic groups. He produced more than 40 videos and 15 books and at one point had the largest camp in the world with more than 5,000 campers each summer.

Gongs and drums, and banners and flags make the army hear with the same ear and see with the same eye. Thus unified in understanding, the brave cannot advance alone nor the cowardly retreat.

■ *Sun Tzu*

12. RITUALS

The seasoned general cultivates a tribal mentality tapping into one of the strongest impulses of humanity. Since the dawn of time, small bands of related humans have bonded in groups to hunt and survive. We are hard-wired by evolution to value loyalty, to commit to the quest and to practice ritual. A warrior culture thrives when habit becomes routine, routine becomes ritual, and ritual becomes identity. Generals must encourage and protect the rituals that organically arise, for these define the tribal experience.

Athletes embrace ritual in all aspects of competition. Individuals and groups seek the familiar by adopting subtle and overt prescriptive behavior. Rituals help to relax, rituals strengthen ties, rituals empower.

Individual: Each soldier should adopt personal rituals to achieve the highest physical and psychological readiness before battle. Many choose to synchronize naps, with meditation, visualization, pre-game menu and personal music. In addition, serious warriors develop a consistent warm-up sequence of stretching, ball-handling and shooting progressions even before the squad enters the field of battle.

Free throw rituals are critical to success at the line. Repetitive behavior helps to neutralize or prevent anxiety by conjuring the familiar. Breath control, dribble counts, rim focus, hand placement on the ball, silent incantation, knee dip, follow-through are all personalized mechanics that need to be perfectly replicated with each shot.

Team rituals: Team rituals expand into every aspect of hardwood life. From how a team begins and ends practice, to how a team collectively prepares psychologically for combat before a contest, all involve key elements of group ritual. Linking arms, choreographed movement, team chanting, call and response can all trigger ancient instincts that heighten aggression and solidify oneness.

Teams should organize their timeouts to ensure maximum attention by all players. Give careful attention to the seating and standing arrangement on the bench. As they prepare to resume combat, teams should break their huddles with the verbalization of a mission word(s). Thus is the unifying power of ritual.

Locker rooms are appropriate places to institute rituals for team cohesion. Many armies adopt the ritual of physically touching a symbol, sign or logo strategically located above an exit door.

Another ritual used in some locker rooms involves placing a full length mirror on the exit door. Each time a warrior exits he is forced to literally look himself in the mirror. Place a statement or question above the mirror:

Team Guy or Me Guy?
Check Your EGO
This, This, These
Selfless Service
Smart and Hard (Head and Heart)

Pre and Post Game

Generals should adhere to a predictable ritual of pre-game instruction. Choose a standard time to enter the locker room. The team should be completely in uniform and ready for your final reminders of game-plan details. If possible, no one should be in the field of vision of the troops except the general when he/she is addressing them because troops are easily distracted by fidgeting, shifting body weight, jangling of keys, coughing and other unconscious body movements. Always solicit additional comments from any of your trusted advisers, and ask if the troops have any questions.

Post-game should also include some standard rituals. No one should be undressing or taking off their sneakers until your remarks are finished. Once again allow your officers to provide observations when you are finished with your imme-diate feedback.

Both winning and losing locker rooms can be emotional. Be aware that there is a mythical quota on how many times a coach can effectively "go ballistic" on his or her team during the year before the troops tune out or mutiny.

Fire: Fire is primal, elemental and purifying. Under highly supervised conditions, the use of fire can produce dramatic symbolic results. Burn a pair of sneakers, old uniforms, last year's scorebook, an effigy of an opponent's mascot. A team that circles around a small bonfire under the winter stars will experience powerful primal connections with every member of the tribe.

FLOOR GENERAL

Dean Smith: (career:1953-1997)

Perhaps the most creative basketball technician to ever walk the sidelines, Dean Smith's impact on the sport of basketball was vast and indelible. Pointing to the assist man after a score, implementing the 'tired signal' by tapping one's head to get a quick rest, huddling before foul shots, having the bench stand up to acknowledge someone coming out of a game, handing a towel to the player coming out of the game by his replacement were all first modeled by Tar Heel players. Strategically, Coach Smith popularized the Carolina fast break, the 'point zone,' the 'run and jump,' double teaming the pick and roll, and expanding on John McClendon's 4-corner stall. The Carolina team motto is PLAY HARD, PLAY SMART, PLAY TOGETHER. More importantly, Dean Smith was willing to take controversial stands on a number of social issues. He recruited Charlie Scott, the school's first black player, in 1966. He campaigned to end the death penalty in North Carolina and he was an outspoken critic of nuclear proliferation.

The general who advances without coveting fame and retreats without fearing disgrace, whose only thought is to protect his country and do good service for his sovereign, is the jewel of the kingdom.

■ *Sun Tzu*

13. RANDOM ANCIENT WISDOM

The three most important stats are charges, floor burns and stitches. Everything else will take care of itself.

On good teams there are players who are willing to do the dirty work. On great teams every player is willing to do the dirty work.

Announce a practice MVP each night.

Basketball is not a democracy – scorers are part of the aristocracy.

Press the country teams, zone the city teams.

Don't spook your shooters. They need continual and confident reassurance.

Smiling instinctively relaxes the entire body. Make a player
smile before a critical foul shot.

During practice, players on the sideline or under the basket
should coach and correct their teammates during competitive
drills.

Try to incorporate some original team vocabulary. There's
more buy- in by the players:

> ***Train wrecks*** – (charges)

> ***Womb*** – (key or paint)

> ***Magnetic Line*** – (imaginary line down middle of key that
> pulls help-side defenders into position)

> **Half court *hover*** – (last man on fast break hovers near
> half court in case there is a quick turn-
> over. This prevents a 'run-out' by the
> opponent.)

> ***Tar pits*** – (The four corners of the ½ court where the ball
> goes to die in a trap)

One strategy to help a slumping shooter is to make him or her
shoot for 10 or 15 minutes with their opposite hand. When
they return to their dominant hand, the brain sometimes
resets.

Also, jump shooters should consciously increase the height of their jump to achieve a nanosecond longer for target adjustment.

Think about the arrangement of players and coaches on your bench. Put your top two subs on either side of you. They become more involved and you can address them with more detailed instruction before insertion. Your defensive coach should locate closer to the half-court where defense is being played in each half.

Appoint captains. No voting. Know who you want to be the extension of yourself on the floor.

Loud, supportive chatter energizes a practice.

Coach ticked off (have an edge.)

Look your players in the eyes as they walk onto the practice floor. Eyes are the windows to the soul. You can sometimes sense a problem.

Address your players by their first names. Avoid using just their last name. It carries a hint of disrespect.

Defenses can control four areas:

1. Second shots
2. Penetration
3. Low post scoring (quick doubles)
4. Fast break points

When a post player is double-teamed have him drag the double team away from the basket with a quick dribble or two. This creates more passing room to hit cutters as well as create more distance for the defense to recover during ball reversal.

Though initially painful and embarrassing, getting cut can sometimes free a young person to pursue other interests and passions that will ultimately be more rewarding than languishing at the end of a bench or rotting on the sidelines during practice.

On a designed, quick hitting back-door play, a coach can contribute to its execution by screaming to his player at just the right moment to "COME GET IT". The defender often overplays with more aggressiveness.

Some savvy coaches instruct their teams to use the last digit on the score clock to call out-of-bounds plays. No hand signals or verbal communication is needed.

Instead of splitting a 1-3-1 half court trap or extended 1-3-1 zone with a conventional 2-1-2 alignment - match up on the perimeter with three players. It sounds counter-intuitive but it's far easier to swing the ball and distort the zone.

The head coach should wear a different color shirt or a loud tie so the players on the floor can quickly locate him in the heat of battle.

Code some of your plays by cities in a particular state:

Pittsburgh, Philly, Scranton = SAME PLAY

Practice fouling deliberately for end of game situations and have both a verbal call and a hand signal to initiate it.

Setting a point total as a defensive goal is deceptive and pointless. Game tempos vary dramatically for a number of reasons. Your defensive goal should simply be to stop each individual possession.

An opponent's shooting percentage is determined by how many shots were made *uncomfortable* or *unnatural* (contested, rushed, deeper than normal, wrong player, unfamiliar spots, circus wigglers etc.)

Offensive M . . . – The purposeless, auto-erotic display of stationary ball handling. It makes the dribbler feel good, but no one else benefits.

Greatness is not about "want to," it's about "need to."

A legitimate question to a player whose effort is consistently unsatisfactory: "Is this the way you want to be remembered by your coaches and teammates?"

A serious commitment to cardio improvement can increase one's scoring average by 3 to 5 points in a given year.

Good teams take pride in being able to play several styles of defense. There are offensive answers to every defense, but most teams don't have answers to all defenses.

Two quick handclaps from a pt. guard to demand the ball can be heard in the top row of an arena.

Insist on a relay chain among players on the floor when a set play or defensive change is communicated from the bench.

Failure is an event, not a person. Lose the game, not your dignity.

Charlie the Tuna – Know which players taste good, and which players have good taste. Some very effective players do not pass the eye test but help you win. Some players look awesome but don't deliver in critical situations.

TAKE MY ARMY FROM ME - When battle-tested warriors assume complete ownership of the goals, values, discipline and culture cultivated by a great leader, they have reached the highest plane in the competitive realm. The general can then step back and admire his masterpiece, for he is no longer needed.

THE LEGEND OF MOON TZU

It is believed that Moon Tzu was born sometime in the middle of the 20th century in a small town near the foothills of the Allegheny Mountains. According to legend, he assumed command of a small militia at the age of twenty-two. During his first campaign his troops suffered devastating losses in twenty of their first twenty two battles. His only victories that year came at the expense of a neighboring principality who were subdued by the narrowest of margins - once in overtime and once on a last second kill-shot from the unlikeliest of archers. Eventually, warriors of great renown and prowess began to fill the ranks of his growing army as they marched across the hills of his homeland torching every hostile gym. Smoke and wailing rose skyward as his victorious troops marched homeward with the spoils of war.

After eight years of increasingly ruthless plunder, Moon Tzu suddenly withdrew for three years from his martial life of slaughter to seek wisdom through meditation. He embarked on a spiritual trek to the mystical city of siren songs. One winter night, Moon Tzu heard a voice that beckoned him to "stare into the reflecting pool." Its cryptic meaning was slowly unraveled. Destiny demanded that he resume leading young warriors into hardwood combat. Shortly thereafter, Moon Tzu assumed command of an army in the southern region of the empire, and for the next thirty years refined the craft of basketball warfare during his quest for the ever elusive GOLD BALL.

After the final battle of his last campaign, Moon Tzu returned alone to his homeland where it is said he succumbed to the mortal wound inflicted in the final seconds of that last devastating defeat. Rumors, however, have circulated for years of occasional sightings on winter nights of a stooped, grizzled phantom hobbling down the bleacher steps of crowded high school gymnasiums before disappearing into the snow like the ghost-warriors spoken of in ancient fables.

SUN TZU quotation sources:

http://www.artofwarquotes.com/

http://www.goodreads.com/work/quotes/3200649-s-nzi-b-ngf

http://www.military-quotes.com/Sun-Tzu.htm

Sun Tzu, The Art of War, James Trapp – Trans. Amber Books LTD. United Kingdom. 2011.

FLOOR GENERAL sources consulted:

Phog Allen   http://kuhistory.com/articles/phogs-firsfarewell/

http://www.nabc.org/about/about-history-keydates.html

Clair Bee   Teitel Jon. "He put the "Bee" in Basketball: CHD remembers Hall of Fame coach Clair Bee" COLLEGE HOOPS DAILY. March 5, 2014.

http://www.hoophall.com/halloffamers/bhof-clair-bee.html

Hank Iba   ESPN, ed. (2009). ESPN College Basketball Encyclopedia: The Complete History of the Men's Game. New York, NY: ESPN Books. p. 544. ISBN 978- 0-345-51392-2.

Goldpapaer, Sam. "Henry Iba. 88, A Top Coach in Basketball." New York Times. January, 16, 1993.

John Mclendon   Merlino, Tom. <u>The Crossover: A Brief History of Basketball and Race, from James Naismith to LeBron James</u>. E-book. July 10, 2001.

<u>Black Magic</u>. ESPN FILMS. Shoot the Moon Productions. March 2008.

Tex Winter   Coffey, Wayne. "Master Mind: Meet Tex Winter, the man behind Phil Jackson's Triangle offense". New York Daily News. 15 March 2014).

Pete Newell   <u>Pete Newell Big Man Camp</u>, petenewell-bigmancamp.com, accessed October 9, 2010.

Weber, Bruce. <u>Pete Newell, Basketball Coach and Innovator, Dies at 93.</u> The New York Times. Nov. 17, 2008.

Ed McCluskey   *Raykie, Jim.* "Farrell High Legend McCluskey inducted into WPIAL Hall of Fame." Sharon Herald. Jun 20, 2008.

Pat Head Summitt Pat Summitt Bio - University of Tennessee Official Athletic Site. http://www.utsports.com/sports/w-baskbl/mtt/summitt_pat00.html.

Pete Carril The Smart Take from the Strong: The Basketball Philosophy of Pete Carill ...https://www.amazon.com/Smart-Take-Strong BasketbalPhilosophy/.../0803264488

Princeton Motion Offense - HoopTactics Basketball Offensive Strategies hooptactics.net/premium/offense/motion-offense/princeton.php.

Dick Bennett Cartagena, Tony. "Dick Bennett built the Foundation of Wisconsin Basketball." ESPN ... www.espn.com/blog/ .../the-five-pillars-of-wisconsin-basketball-built-by-dick-bennett.

Morgan Wooten Halley, Jim. Morgan Wooten Helped Shape Modern High School Basketball, USA TODAY Sports Published 4:57 p.m. ET May 1, 2013 | Updated 9:21 a.m. ET May 2, 2013.

Don Meyer Olney, Buster (May 18, 2014). "Don Meyer dies at age of 69". ESPN.com. Retrieved March 28, 2017.

Climer, David (May 18, 2014) "Don Meyer was a coach of life, not just basketball." Tennessean.com. Retrieved March 29, 2017.

Dean Smith   Larivere, David (February 8, 2015). "Dean Smith, One of the Greatest Innovators In College Basketball, deat At 83" *Forbes*. <u>*Archived*</u> *from the original on February 9, 2015.*

Wolff, Alexander. *"The Father of Invention: Seven Innovations"*. Sports Illustrated.

Dean Smith: The 1997 Sports Illustrated Sportsman of the Year. Retrieved October 29, 2006.

Puma, Mike. (May 18, 2006). <u>*"The Dean of College Hoops"*</u>. ESPN. *Retrieved October 29, 2006.*

CPSIA information can be obtained
at www.ICGtesting.com
Printed in the USA
BVOW08s1321310817
493593BV00001B/19/P